THE SECOND WORLD WAR IN THE AIR
IN PHOTOGRAPHS

1942

L. ARCHARD

AMBERLEY

First published 2014

Amberley Publishing
The Hill, Stroud
Gloucestershire, GL5 4EP

www.amberley-books.com

Copyright © L. Archard, 2014

The right of L. Archard to be identified as the Author of this work has
been asserted in accordance with the
Copyrights, Designs and Patents Act 1988.

British Library Cataloguing in Publication Data.
A catalogue record for this book is available from the British Library.

ISBN 978 1 4456 2246 0 (print)
ISBN 978 1 4456 2269 9 (ebook)

Typesetting and Origination by Amberley Publishing.
Printed in Great Britain.

Introduction

As 1942 started, the Japanese campaign in the Far East continued unabated. At the start of January, the Japanese were pushing forward in the Philippines, Malaya, Burma and Java. British troops were withdrawing back through Malaya towards Singapore, and on 20 January, Japanese aircraft bombed Singapore as their troops approached the city. In early February, the Japanese bombed Port Moresby on New Guinea, and now started to pose a threat to northern Australia. Later in the month, Japanese forces in Thailand pushed into Burma in an attempt to cut off the so-called Burma Road, a route for transporting supplies to the Chinese forces fighting the Japanese, which terminated in the south-western city of Kunming in Yunnan Province. In an attempt to continue supplying the Chinese, an air route was set up from Assam in the north-east of India, flying over the eastern end of the Himalayas ('the Hump').

Meanwhile, in the Mediterranean, the air attacks on Malta continued, with the tonnage of bombs dropped on the island during the war estimated at being double that dropped on London. In the English Channel, the German pocket battleships *Scharnhorst* and *Gneisenau*, accompanied by the cruiser *Prinz Eugen*, left the French Atlantic port of Brest and successfully ran the gauntlet of the English Channel on 11 February. The ships escaped detection until they were approaching the Straits of Dover, but once they had been detected, a series of attacks by air and sea were launched to stop them. Unfortunately, support from Luftwaffe fighter squadrons stationed in northern France as well as the ships' own anti-aircraft guns made this a costly mission; Lieutenant-Commander Eugene Esmond led a force of Fleet Air Arm Swordfish torpedo bombers against the German ships, and only five of the eighteen crew members involved survived, Esmonde himself winning a posthumous Victoria Cross for his courage in leading the attack.

Later in February, the Japanese launched a bombing raid against Darwin, in Australia's Northern Territories, and at the start of March they attacked the airfield and harbour at Broome, Western Australia. At the end of March, as the RAF strategic bombing campaign against Germany began to build up momentum, there was a heavy bombing raid against the city of Lübeck. A historic city that had once been a member of the medieval Hanseatic League, Lübeck was chiefly a cultural centre, and many Germans, including Hitler himself, were outraged at its destruction; the city had had many ancient wooden buildings, which had been especially vulnerable to the RAF's use of incendiary bombs. In retaliation, the Germans planned a series of attacks against British cities of similar cultural importance, the so-called Baedeker Raids, named after the well-known German tourist guide to Britain, which was supposedly used to pick the list of targets. Among the cities attacked were Canterbury, Norwich, Cambridge, York and Exeter; some important buildings were destroyed, including the York Guildhall and Bath's Assembly Rooms, and Norwich, Exeter and Canterbury cathedrals were damaged, as was York Minster.

In April, US forces achieved a measure of retaliation for the Pearl Harbor attack by mounting the so-called Doolittle Raid. Flying B-25 Mitchell bombers from the aircraft carrier USS *Hornet*, Lieutenant-Colonel James Doolittle and his crews bombed targets in the Japanese cities of Nagoya, Yokohama and Tokyo, among others. The targets in Tokyo included an oil tank facility, a steel mill and several power plants, while in Yokusuka a bomb from one of the B-25s hit a light aircraft carrier nearing completion in a shipyard. Six schools and an army hospital were also hit. The raiders encountered only light anti-aircraft fire and a few enemy fighters over Japan. Because the twin-engined Mitchells could not be landed back on the aircraft carrier (there had been some debate about whether they would be too heavy to even take off), they were flown over Japan and on into China, where the crews crash-landed in the hope that friendly Chinese forces would help them get home. By and large, this is what happened, sixty-nine of the eighty crewmen returning safely; the rest were captured or killed, or, in the case of one crew, interned in the Soviet Union after landing in eastern Siberia. They were not the only American pilots in China; the so-called Flying Tigers (officially known as the AVG, American Volunteer Group) were flying their P-40 fighters in support of the Chinese forces fighting the Japanese. Their commander, Claire Chennault, had been in China since 1937, when he had been hired to organise an air force for the country, but American servicemen (reserve officers and enlisted men) had only been permitted to volunteer to join Chennault's force in April 1941. Japanese forces, meanwhile, mounted a series of raids against the island of Ceylon (now Sri Lanka), bombing the city of Trincomalee and sinking several warships of the Royal Navy and the Royal Australian Navy off the coast. May saw the Battle of the Coral Sea. A Japanese carrier group supporting an attack on the island of Tulagi in the Gilbert Islands (part of a plan to capture Port Moresby) was itself attacked by the US Navy. The Americans lost the aircraft carrier USS *Lexington* while the USS *Yorktown* was damaged; the Japanese aircraft carrier *Shokaku* was damaged badly enough to require two months of repairs. Although the Japanese arguably came out of the Battle of the Coral Sea the victors, the Port Moresby operation was cancelled.

At the end of May, the RAF marked a milestone in the development of the bombing campaign against Germany: the first Thousand-Bomber raid. Operation Millennium was a major demonstration of the area bombing techniques that RAF Bomber Command hoped would cripple the Germans' will and ability to carry on the war. Although it could be argued that the scale of the Thousand-Bomber raids was entirely different, the effects of bombing on civilian populations until this point show that this was not a given. The propaganda value of the raids, however, meant that another was launched in early June, this time against the city of Essen, the centre of the German industrial heartland, the Ruhr Valley. In July, a heavy attack would be made using incendiaries against Hamburg, another city that would suffer heavily from bombing during the war. Bomber Command's standard bomb load for area attacks (code-named 'Usual') was a 4,000-lb high-capacity bomb (known as a 'Cookie') and 30-lb incendiary bombs; the idea was that blast damage from the explosion of the Cookie would help to spread the fires caused by the incendiaries, particularly by blowing the roof tiles from buildings so that the incendiaries could land inside them. The Cookie could be a dangerous load to carry; air rushing over the detonator in the nose could cause it to explode, even if it had been jettisoned without being armed, and if it was dropped below 6,000 feet, the blast would damage the aircraft.

Because of its unobstructed bomb bay, the Lancaster was the only one of the three four-engine heavy bombers in service with the RAF that could carry the 4,000-lb bomb. The Lancaster, Roy Chadwick's highly successful redesign of the troubled Avro Manchester, using four Rolls-Royce Merlin engines, first started to come into service in early 1942 with the RAF's No. 44 Squadron. Carrying seven crew members, the Lancaster would become the backbone of Bomber Command, replacing the Short Stirling and Handley Page Halifax in the offensive against Germany. Another famous RAF aircraft that came into widespread service in 1942 was the De Havilland Mosquito, the 'Wooden Wonder'. Made of light balsa and birch wood, and powered by two Rolls-Royce Merlin engines, the Mosquito was one of the fastest operational aircraft in the world when it first came into service, and was used as a high-altitude photograph reconnaissance aircraft, although later in the year it began to see use as a high-speed low- and medium-altitude bomber and as a night fighter.

At the start of June, the Japanese began to launch air raids against the Aleutian Islands, which run in a chain south and east from the coast of Alaska into the Barents Sea. Later in the month, the Japanese would occupy the islands of Attu and Kiska. However, events far to the south would prove to be of greater significance. On 3 June, the Battle of Midway started, with ineffective attacks by land-based B-17 bombers against the Japanese naval force approaching the island. The following day, aircraft from the three American aircraft carriers in the vicinity of the island (alerted to Japanese intentions by American code-breakers), USS *Hornet*, USS *Yorktown* and USS *Enterprise*, located and attacked the Japanese carrier force. The decks of the Japanese ships *Akagi*, *Kaga* and *Soryu* were crowded with fuelling lines, bombs and torpedoes, and the American attacks soon reduced them to blazing hulks. The fourth carrier in the Japanese force, *Hiryu*, launched an attack that successfully damaged the USS *Yorktown* so badly that it had to be abandoned, but on 4 June aircraft from the remaining American carriers located and destroyed *Hiryu* as well. The Japanese navy had been dealt a devastating blow. In another moment of enormous significance, later in June the Manhattan Project would start work on the development of the atomic bomb. In December, a team led by Italian physicist Enrico Fermi started the first nuclear chain reaction below the bleachers at Stagg Field at the University of Chicago. President Roosevelt was informed in a coded message that read, 'The Italian navigator has landed in the new world.' There were other moments of technical development in 1942 as well; in July, the Germans flew the third prototype of the Messerschmitt Me

262 (the world's first operational jet fighter) using only its Junkers Jumo 004 engines, although engine reliability issues would continue to plague the project, while at the start of October there was the first successful launch of an A4 rocket (the technical name for what would become known as the V2) at the test facility at Peenemünde on Germany's Baltic coast; the rocket flew for 147 km and reached a height of 84.5 km, making it the first man-made object to reach space.

The day of 4 July saw the first American bombing raid against German-occupied Europe, an attack by American crews flying American-made RAF Havoc twin-engined bombers against an airfield in the Netherlands. Although there were B-17 heavy bombardment groups based in the UK, the first B-17 raid wasn't until 17 August, when a raid was mounted against the Sotteville marshalling yards outside Rouen in Normandy. At the start of August, US forces began their campaign to retake the island of Guadalcanal in the Solomon Islands, east of Papua New Guinea. Air power would play a significant role in the campaign, with the heavily contested airfield on the island, Henderson Field, key to preventing the Japanese from gaining air superiority over Guadalcanal. The campaign would continue until November, when the last Japanese attempt to land enough troops to eject the Americans failed. Later in August, a Japanese seaplane would drop incendiary bombs on the Pacific coast state of Oregon, starting a forest fire, in one of the only bombing raids on the mainland United States during the Second World War. In the Mediterranean, meanwhile, one of the Malta convoys was coming under particularly intense attack from both the air and the sea, resulting in the sinking of the aircraft carrier HMS *Eagle*, part of the convoy escort, by a German U-boat. On 15 April, King George VI had awarded the island of Malta the George Cross, Britain's highest civilian medal for gallantry, in tribute to its resilience in the face of German and Italian bombing.

Late in August, the Luftwaffe began heavily bombing the city of Stalingrad, on the Volga River in the south of the Soviet Union, as ground troops from the German Sixth Army approached. The Battle of Stalingrad proper would begin in early September when the German troops entered the suburbs of the city. The city would be razed to the ground, partly by artillery and partly by German air power, as the Luftwaffe carried out close air support missions as well as more general bombing missions and attempts to interdict the stream of supplies coming across the Volga to the embattled Soviet troops in the city. As the tactical situation changed and the Germans were encircled and cut off in the ruins of Stalingrad, the Luftwaffe would attempt to fly in supplies to the Sixth Army.

At the end of October and into November 1942, General Montgomery's Eighth Army fought the Second Battle of El Alamein against the Afrika Korps. Obviously, the main focus of the battle was on the ground forces, but as the German and Italian front line crumbled and the troops began to pull back from Egypt, the Desert Air Force played a key role in hastening that process. The Desert Air Force attacked the retreating Axis troops and their supply dumps as well as preventing the Luftwaffe from intervening in the battle. There were two particularly key missions, in which two oil tankers, the *Tergestea* and the *Proserpina*, were sunk in Tobruk harbour, removing any hope that Rommel had of being able to refuel his tanks and other vehicles. Elsewhere in North

Africa, at the start of November, Operation Torch, the Allied invasion of Morocco and Algeria (controlled by the pro-German Vichy regime in France), began. The Vichy French forces in the area had about 500 aircraft, roughly half of which were effective Dewoitine D.520 fighters, and the Germans launched bombing missions against the invasion forces as well; in order to counter this, the invasion force that had set sail from the United States included several aircraft carriers, landing US P-40 fighters at Port Lyautey in Morocco while Supermarine Seafire fighters also operated in the area, having been transported by sea and assembled at Gibraltar.

The year 1942 would prove to be something of a turning point in the Second World War generally. After the war, Churchill would say, 'Before Alamein we never had a victory. After Alamein, we never had a defeat.' In terms of the war in the air, the offensive capability of the Imperial Japanese Navy had been crippled by the loss of its aircraft carriers at the Battle of Midway, although the Japanese would continue to stubbornly defend their conquests, while in Europe and the Mediterranean, the remorseless bombing of Malta drew to a close as the Germans pulled out of North Africa, and the bombing of Britain too died away as German resources were concentrated on the Eastern Front. However, the development of German rocket technology meant that the threat had not disappeared completely.

January

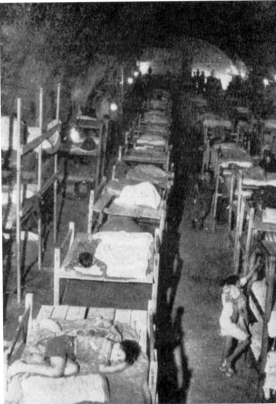

Above left: The entrance to an air-raid shelter on Malta, dug deep into the island's rock.

Above right: Inside an air-raid shelter on Malta. The original caption for this photograph describes the shelter as being one of thirty 'underground galleries of great antiquity'.

The Grand Harbour at Valletta, Malta, under air attack.

Opposite above: A grainy photograph of Kai Tak airfield, Hong Kong, following a bombing raid by Japanese aircraft. Japanese forces invaded Hong Kong on 8 December 1941, but the British colony did not surrender until 25 December.

Opposite below: A clearer view of Hong Kong under attack. The pillar of smoke to the left of the photograph is rising from a bomb exploding on Kai Tak airfield.

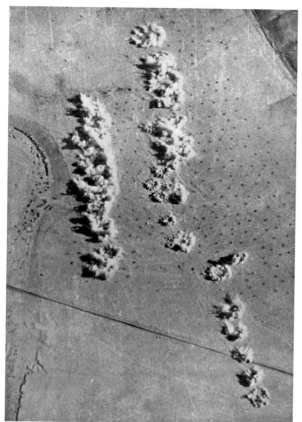

Left: A photograph showing an RAF bombing raid against an ammunition dump concealed in the Western Desert of Libya. Supply was one of Rommel's weaknesses as a general, not helped in North Africa by the activities of the RAF and the Royal Navy.

Below: Martin Maryland bombers of the Desert Air Force being loaded with bombs in preparation for another raid against the Axis forces in Libya. 'Maryland' was the name given by the British to the Martin Model 167 bomber; originally ordered by the French as part of their build-up, the undelivered portion of the order went to Britain after the fall of France and, with a further British order, was deployed to North Africa.

Bombs bursting in the Mediterranean between the battleship HMS *Royal Sovereign* and the aircraft carrier HMS *Eagle*. In December 1941, Field Marshal Albert Kesselring led Luftflotte 2 to the Mediterranean theatre, becoming German Commander-in-Chief South. This led to a dramatic upsurge in German air activity as Kesselring aimed to achieve local air superiority and neutralise Malta.

A blurry photograph showing an Axis merchant ship under attack by an RAF aircraft in the Mediterranean. The German forces in North Africa depended on supplies, particularly fuel, shipped across the Mediterranean, and to protect those supply routes, Malta had to be neutralised – the island was a key base for both RAF and Royal Navy aircraft and the Royal Navy's submarines.

Two photographs showing a crashed Heinkel He 111 somewhere in Britain fitted with a device extending from one wing tip to the other to protect the aircraft from barrage balloon cables.

The crew of a cruiser bringing up the rear of a convoy bound for northern Russia can be seen using a steam jet to clear ice from the capstan and chains at the bow of the ship. Although the weather made conditions for the crews of ships on this route pretty miserable, it also sheltered the ships to a certain extent from German air attacks launched from bases in Norway.

However, the Germans did launch as many attacks as they could on the convoys, particularly as they came close to the end of their voyages to the northern Soviet ports of Murmansk and Arkhangelsk. This photograph shows Soviet naval gunners examining the wreckage of a Junkers Ju 88 brought down on the coast of the Barents Sea.

Left: The results of Allied attempts to supply the Soviet armed forces. This photograph, which looks to have been altered or adjusted in some way, shows a group of Soviet pilots gathered around a Curtiss P-40 Tomahawk fighter supplied by the US. Armed, in its earlier models, with six machine guns, the Tomahawk was an effective fighter used by the US forces in the Far East and by the volunteer pilots of the Flying Tigers in China, as well as by the Desert Air Force in Libya and the Soviet forces.

Below: A Petlyakov Pe-2 bomber of the Soviet air force is prepared for a raid against the Germans, retreating before a counteroffensive led by General Zhukov. Designed as a dive-bomber, the Pe-2 was fast enough to evade Luftwaffe fighters and durable enough to carry out accurate attacks on ground targets.

Above: On 20 January, Japanese aircraft bombed Singapore as their troops approached the city down the Malay Peninsula. This photograph shows repairs to bomb damage in a square in the city.

Right: A civilian casualty of the Japanese bombing is manoeuvred out of a house on a stretcher and on to a lorry carrying the initials of the Singapore Municipal Council.

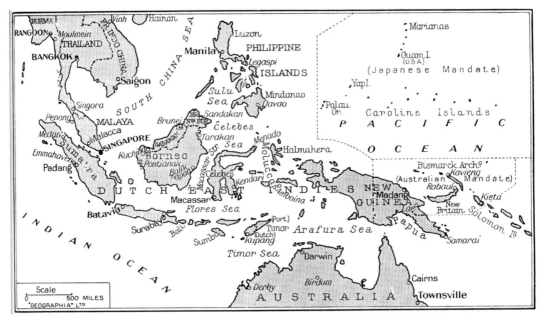

By the end of January 1942, Allied forces had evacuated Malaya. The Japanese threatened Singapore and Rangoon (following the fall of Moulmein); American troops were under siege in the Bataan Peninsula in the Philippines; and there was fighting in New Guinea, the Solomon Islands and Indonesia (labelled the Dutch East Indies on this map).

February

A vivid drawing by an RAF squadron leader showing an attack by RAF Curtiss P-40 Tomahawk fighters on an Axis supply column in the Libyan desert.

These two photographs show a Short Sunderland flying boat forced down in the Mediterranean off the Libyan coast. The Sunderland remained afloat for some two and a half hours after it came down. It was attacked by two Messerschmitt fighters; the Sunderland, known to the Germans as the Flying Porcupine for its eighteen machine guns in multiple turrets, could often hold its own against enemy aircraft.

Civilians in Malta clearing away the debris from the explosion of a bomb. By the end of 1941, Malta had suffered more than 1,000 bombing raids by Axis aircraft and would be one of the areas most intensively bombed during the war.

The object of the exercise. Malta was a key British base in the Mediterranean for submarines and aircraft, but it was important for British operations in the Mediterranean more generally as well. This photograph shows troops being offloaded at the Grand Harbour, Valletta.

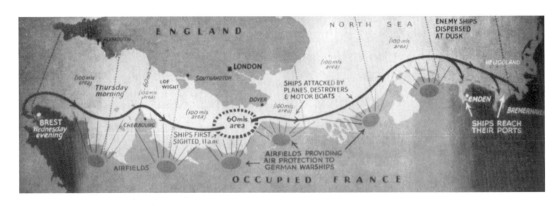

Above left: Sub-Lieutenant E. Lee was the only survivor out of eighteen Fleet Air Arm Swordfish pilots who went out to attack the German warships. The others were wounded or killed.

Above right: Lieutenant-Commander Esmonde, the leader of the Swordfish attack on *Scharnhorst* and *Gneisenau*, failed to return, but was awarded a posthumous Victoria Cross for courage.

Opposite above: The Channel Dash. On 12 February 1942, the pocket battleships *Scharnhorst* and *Gneisenau*, accompanied by the heavy cruiser *Prinz Eugen*, made a fast voyage through the English Channel from the French Atlantic port of Brest to Germany.

Opposite below: A group photograph of some Bristol Blenheim bomber pilots who attacked German ships as they travelled through the English Channel. The ships themselves were well armed with anti-aircraft guns and also had cover from Luftwaffe fighter squadrons in northern France, so the British pilots suffered heavy casualties.

Dutch Air Force personnel are met on their arrival in Singapore to help the British forces defending the island. The Japanese attack on the oil-rich Dutch East Indies (now Indonesia) brought the Dutch into the war in the Far East.

Bombers of the Royal Netherlands Air Force being loaded with bombs at an airfield somewhere in Indonesia prior to launching a raid to help the beleaguered defenders of Singapore.

The wreckage of the jetty at Darwin, in Australia's Northern Territories. The city, a key base for attempts to defend the Dutch East Indies, was bombed heavily by Japanese forces on 19 February.

Japanese army Mitsubishi bombers warming up on an airfield in northern China.

Bomb damage in Rangoon, in what was then the British colony of Burma. The Japanese attacked Burma from Thailand, aiming to capture Rangoon and thus close the route known as the Burma Road, which led to the city of Kunming in China's south-western Yunnan Province, and was used by Britain to send supplies to the Chinese forces fighting the Japanese.

On the night of 27/28 February 1942, British paratroopers jumped into Occupied France to attack the German Würzburg radar facility at Bruneval, on the coast near Le Havre. Prisoners and components from the radar equipment were taken back to Britain. These photographs show some of the paratroopers being transported back by ship, as well as some of the prisoners taken in the raid. Würzburg radar was a key part of the German defences against RAF night bomber attacks.

The bomb-shattered ruins of Tripoli, a major port on the North African coast, used to supply Rommel's Afrika Korps. Bombing the port where the supplies were unloaded as well as attempting to sink the merchant ships at sea was an important part of depriving the Afrika Korps of the supplies, especially fuel, it needed.

March

An aerial photograph of Wotje Atoll, in what were then the Gilbert and Marshall Islands in the mid-Pacific to the north-east of Australia. Smoke can be seen rising after a raid by US naval aircraft and bombardment by US warships.

Above: Refuelling and rearming aircraft on the deck of a US Navy aircraft carrier, following an attack by American forces on the Gilbert Islands. The islands had been invaded by the Japanese on the same day as the attack on Pearl Harbor, and were completely occupied within a few days.

Left: Damage to an American warship caused by a Japanese bomb.

Two photographs showing
damage inflicted in a bombing
raid on the Renault works
at Billancourt, outside Paris;
the factory was being used
to produce tanks for the
occupying Germans.

A blimp of the US Navy dropping depth charges while on an anti-submarine patrol. In the first months of 1942, German submarines began attacking shipping off the US East Coast. At night, the ships, not in convoy, were easy to pick out against the city lights, as there was no blackout. Between 13 January and 6 February, the first U-boats sank 156,939 tonnes of shipping without loss. More submarines would follow.

Opposite above: The construction of U-boat pens on the French Atlantic coast. These pens, constructed by the Organisation Todt, would prove to be almost impervious to Allied bombing when complete, and protected the German U-boats from attack while in port.

Opposite below: USAAF men photographed beside a B-17 Flying Fortress in northern Australia. This picture was taken not long before the crew set off for a mission to attack Japanese positions at Koepang airport on the island of Timor, Indonesia.

A Consolidated Catalina flying boat of the RAF's Coastal Command sitting in the shadow of the Rock of Gibraltar. German U-boat activity in the Mediterranean was a serious problem, and the patrolling flying boats were as much help there as in the North Atlantic.

Right: The crew of a Coastal Command Catalina flying boat undergo a kit inspection before they take off on patrol, giving us an idea of the amount of equipment needed to mount patrols lasting many hours over the open sea.

Below: Lookouts on board an aircraft carrier watch for submarines. Vitally important to the British campaign in the Mediterranean, the aircraft carriers were particularly vulnerable to submarine attacks.

On 26 March, RAF bombers carried out a raid against the French port of Le Havre. This aerial photograph shows bombs exploding in the docks, although many of them appear to have exploded in the water rather than on the quays.

Bomb damage in Kingsway, the main street in the Maltese capital Valletta.

An aerial photograph of a section of the city of Lübeck, following a raid by the RAF on the night of 28 March. The vast majority of the buildings in this photograph are roofless, as a result of the firestorm caused by the raid. Although Lübeck was a port, it was mainly a cultural centre, a historic Hanseatic city with many medieval timber buildings, and many Germans were outraged by its destruction.

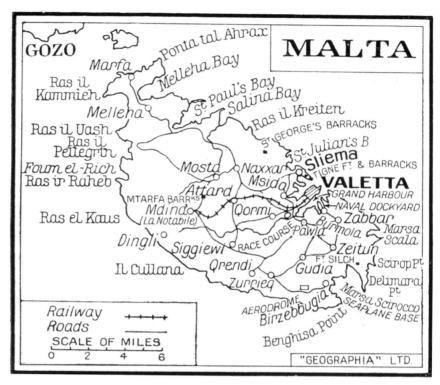

A map of Malta, showing some of the military facilities, including the naval dockyard and various barracks, that made the island so important.

A very vivid artist's impression of a German air raid over the Grand Harbour, Valletta. The constant aerial bombardment took a heavy toll on both Maltese civilians and the British forces defending the island.

April

A U-boat entering the protection of one of the bomb-proof pens on the French Atlantic coast.

Two photographs showing the pilots of the American Volunteer Group (AVG), better known as the Flying Tigers, American military volunteers who flew Curtiss P-40 fighters against the Japanese from bases in south-western China and in Burma, before it fell to the Japanese.

The airfield of Salamaua, Papua New Guinea, on fire following a Japanese air raid. The island of New Guinea was vital for the defence of northern Australia, and was the scene of heavy fighting between Japanese and Australian forces.

On 18 April, a raid was led by Lieutenant-Colonel James Doolittle against the Japanese cities of Tokyo, Yokosuka, Nagoya, Kobe and Osaka, flying B-25 Marauder bombers from the aircraft carrier USS *Hornet*. This photograph shows one of the Marauders taking off from the *Hornet*. (NARA)

Above left: Doolittle, promoted to brigadier general following the raid, is seen here receiving the Medal of Honor from President Roosevelt. Because the Marauders could not be landed back on the *Hornet*, their crews aimed to crash-land in China. Of the eighty men involved in the raid, sixty-nine were able to make their way home; the rest were interned in the USSR, captured or killed.

Above right: A Chinese anti-aircraft gunner on duty in the city of Chungking. Situated on the Yangtze in Sichuan Province, the city was Chiang Kai-Shek's capital after the fall of Nanjing to the Japanese, and was bombed heavily.

An anti-aircraft gun crew serving with the Chinese forces who were fighting the Japanese in Burma. Guns like this were used to protect the Chinese troops from low-level Japanese air attacks; Japanese superiority in training and equipment were a major problem for the Chinese during the fighting.

Two photographs showing bomb damage in the Bataan Peninsula in the Philippines, in which an American force held out for three months against the Japanese after they had overrun the rest of the islands.

An aerial photograph of Rostock, on the Baltic coast of Germany, following four successive nights of bombing from 23 April. Rostock was the home of the Heinkel aircraft company.

An aerial reconnaissance photograph showing the Heinkel factory at Rostock following the raids. Various buildings in the works damaged in the raids have been identified.

Above left: On the nights of 23 and 24 April, the Luftwaffe targeted Exeter in the first of what would become known as the Baedeker Raids, after the German tourist guide from which the targets were supposedly picked – retaliation on militarily insignificant, but cultural and historic British cities following the bombing of Lübeck. This photograph shows some of the damage in the city centre.

Above right: Bomb damage in Bath, which was attacked by the Luftwaffe on the nights of 25 and 26 April. As well as these and many other houses, the city's famous Georgian Assembly Rooms were burnt out.

Above: The Luftwaffe also visited Norwich, on the night of 27 April. This photograph shows the damage to the Old Boar's Head, a historic inn that dated back to the fifteenth century.

Left: A further Baedeker Raid on the night of 28/29 April targeted York. This photograph shows the city's Guildhall in flames.

A B18 Bolo training aircraft being loaded with practice bombs at a training school for bombardiers in the US. The USAAF was now rapidly building up its strength, with the first groups of what would become the Eighth Air Force preparing to deploy to Britain.

May

The aircraft carrier USS *Lexington* sinking after having been hit by bombs and torpedoes from Japanese aircraft on 8 May 1942, during the Battle of the Coral Sea. The *Lexington* was part of the carrier force that was at sea during the Pearl Harbor attack. She was ferrying aircraft to Midway island.

The Japanese aircraft carrier *Shoho* on fire and sinking, following a torpedo attack by US Navy aircraft at the Battle of the Coral Sea. She was the first Japanese aircraft carrier to be sunk during the war.

Another Japanese aircraft carrier is seen with flames pouring out of her, taking evasive action to avoid more torpedoes from US Navy aircraft. This was the fleet carrier *Shokaku*, which survived the battle only to be torpedoed and sunk by a US submarine during the Battle of the Philippine Sea in June 1944.

On 4 May, as part of the so-called Baedeker Raids, there was an early morning attack on the city of Exeter. One of the bombs fell on the south choir aisle of the city's medieval Gothic cathedral, destroying St James's Chapel and the Sacristy.

On 17 May, the German heavy cruiser *Prinz Eugen* was spotted off the coast of Norway by a Coastal Command reconnaissance aircraft. She is seen here with one of her escort of destroyers.

Later that day, a force of Coastal Command aircraft set out to attack the *Prinz Eugen*. Nine of the aircraft failed to return. This photograph shows the crew of one of the Bristol Beaufort torpedo bombers preparing to set off for the attack. Beauforts would be removed from active service in 1942, to be used as training aircraft until they were declared obsolete in 1945.

The RAF's daylight fighter sweeps over northern France continued. The photograph above shows an American volunteer pilot from the third of the Eagle Squadrons, No. 133 Squadron, climbing out of his aircraft after an attack on the Belgian ports of Ostend and Zeebrugge. Formed in late 1940 and the summer of 1941, the Eagle squadrons became the 4th Fighter Group of the US Eighth Air Force on 29 September 1942. The image to the left shows preparations for a raid, with a train of 200-lb bombs being taken to a line of Hurricane fighter bombers waiting among the trees.

Before and after photographs showing the Köln-Nippes railway workshops at Cologne. On the night of 30/31 May 1942, Cologne was the target of Operation Millennium, the first Thousand-Bomber raid, and these photographs shows some of the damage to the city.

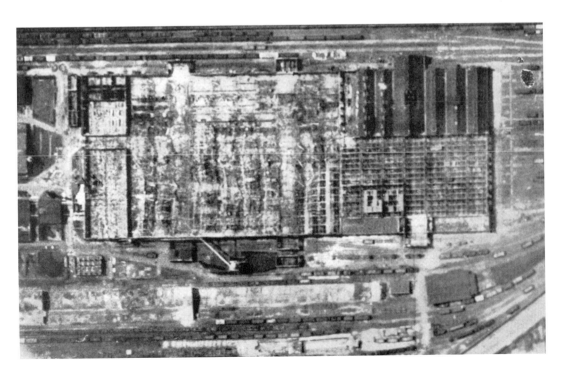

These two propaganda photographs show some of the RAF crews who took part in Operation Millennium. The image above shows a crew from the Royal Canadian Air Force enjoying a cup of tea by their aircraft after being briefed prior to the attack. The image below shows some of the crews on their return.

Another photograph of Cologne following the Thousand-Bomber raid. This one shows the cathedral and the heavily damaged streets of the old town around it. The street running diagonally from the left towards the cathedral is Hohe Strasse, one of the busiest streets in the city. By the end of the war, the cathedral, with its relics of the Three Kings, was one of the few buildings left standing in Cologne.

Two images of Canterbury in Kent, which was attacked by the Luftwaffe in a Baedeker Raid on the night of 31 May, as a reprisal for the destruction of Cologne a few days earlier. The upper image shows bomb damage on Canterbury's High Street, while the image on the left shows the damage to Canterbury Cathedral.

Two images that would be an omen of things to come. These two photographs, taken from a US aircraft carrier in the Pacific, supposedly show a Japanese bomber with its port engine shot away attempting to dive into the aircraft carrier. The upper image shows the damaged bomber passing over a destroyer, while the lower image shows the burning wreckage after the aircraft hit the sea.

June

The crew of the light cruiser HMS *Penelope*, showing the damage caused to her superstructure in attacks by German bombers in the Mediterranean. She had so many shrapnel holes that she was nicknamed HMS *Pepperpot*.

Two photographs of Coastal Command taken from a Whitley bomber, showing bombs dropping on a U-boat in the Bay of Biscay, and then the column of water thrown up by the explosions.

A patch of oil spreading across the water of the Bay of Biscay following the destruction of the submarine.

Aircrew from an RAF bomber squadron flying A-20 Boston light bombers are being briefed in the Operations Room before a mission.

Right: The idea of a thousand bombers was so key to the propaganda aspect of the raids against Cologne and Essen that Bomber Command was scoured for heavy bombers and crews to make up the numbers. The force included Avro Manchester bombers with their unreliable Rolls-Royce Vulture engines; two Manchesters are seen here setting off on a raid.

Below: On the night of 1 June, a second Thousand-Bomber raid was mounted, this time against the city of Essen, a key centre in the industrial area of the Ruhr Valley in western Germany.

Two A-20 Boston bombers of the RAF. The American-made Douglas Boston was used for low-level daylight bombing raids in Occupied Europe, such as those on airfields and power stations.

Opposite top: This image shows the rear gunner of a Soviet bomber firing at a German fighter during a night raid over German-occupied territory.

Opposite bottom: Three pilots of the Soviet air force standing beside the nose of one of the Hawker Hurricane fighters supplied by Britain and used to defend the Arctic port of Murmansk.

Two photographs showing the aftermath of Japanese air raids on Darwin, in the Northern Territories of Australia. The photograph above shows dense clouds of smoke rising from an Australian ship loaded with mines that had been hit; in the foreground, a US Navy destroyer is picking up survivors. The photograph below shows a US troopship on fire after being hit in an attack on 25 June.

A recruitment poster for the US Army Air Force. By the start of 1942, the US was building up the strength of its armed forces following the Pearl Harbor attack in December 1941 and the declarations of war by the Axis powers. (Library of Congress)

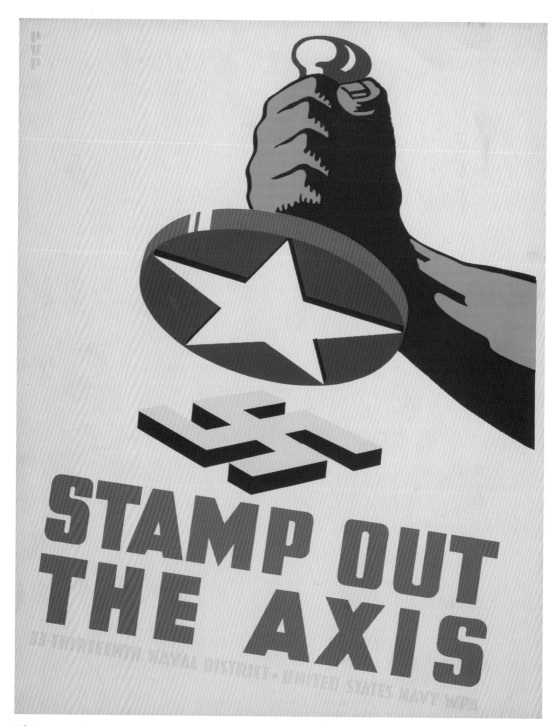

STAMP OUT THE AXIS

This page and opposite: Recruitment posters for the US Navy and US Marines. Both arms would recruit pilots, particularly for service in the Pacific, flying from aircraft carriers and jungle landing strips like Guadalcanal. (Library of Congress)

LET'S GO GET 'EM!

U.S. MARINES

Beck Engraving Co., Phila., Pa., Reqn.—469-1943, 7-11-42, 50M.

This poster shows the other side of American mobilisation: the mobilisation of labour, male and female, to produce the vast quantities of aircraft and munitions that would be needed to win the war. (Library of Congress)

A cartoon produced by the US Army to try and encourage proper maintenance of bombs on wartime air stations. (Library of Congress)

Above: Consolidated B-24 Liberators of the 93rd Bomb Group, which deployed to RAF Alconbury near Huntingdon, in what is now Cambridgeshire, in August and September 1942. (USAF)

Opposite page: Lockheed P-38 Lightning fighters sit on their airfields as the sun rises behind. A Lightning operating from Iceland shot down the first Luftwaffe aircraft to be destroyed by the USAAF, a Focke-Wulf Fw 200 Condor. (USAF)

Above: B-17s en route to their target, flying high above cloud level. (USAF)

Opposite page: German Focke-Wulf Fw 200 Condors patrolled the Atlantic, searching for convoys, but the introduction of catapult aircraft merchantmen (CAM ships) and escort carriers made their job considerably more hazardous.

Above: Dornier Do 17s over the Eastern Front.

Opposite above: Shipping seen below the wing of a banking German aircraft, something Allied seamen must have dreaded, particularly on the Arctic convoys.

Opposite below: A Junkers Ju 52 transport sits on a snow-covered airfield. At the end of 1942, the Luftwaffe's transport pilots were braving the terrible conditions in an attempt to drop supplies to the German forces trapped in Stalingrad.

Two cheerful German airmen putting on the fleece-lined flying suits vital for winter missions on the Eastern Front.

A Luftwaffe bomber crew buckle up in preparation for a night flight over the Eastern Front.

Above: Luftwaffe ground crew scavenging for fuel from abandoned Soviet railway tankers.

Right: An interesting photograph of what must have been a key event of the day on many Luftwaffe bases: preparing to release a weather balloon to check the speed and direction of the wind.

Above: A Junkers Ju 87 Stuka dive-bomber sits on an airfield on Sicily, waiting for its next mission against Malta and the convoys that brought the island much-needed supplies.

Opposite page: Preparing for a mission. Although most of the Luftwaffe's bombers had been diverted elsewhere, enough remained within striking distance of Britain to carry out attacks like the Baedeker Raids.

The leader of a German bombing raid peers out from the bomb-aimer's position through the glazed nose of his Ju 88 aircraft.

An interesting photograph showing a Short Stirling bomber along with the fifty-six personnel needed to operate and maintain it: 1, air crew; 2, meteorological officer; 3, a WAAF parachute packer; 4, flying control officer; 5, flight maintenance; 6, ground servicing; 7, bombing-up team; 8, bomber tractor driver; 9, starter battery operated by (5); 10, oil bowser driver; 11, petrol bowser driver.

Aircrew of RAF Bomber Command being briefed prior to an attack on the city of Bremen on 25 June.

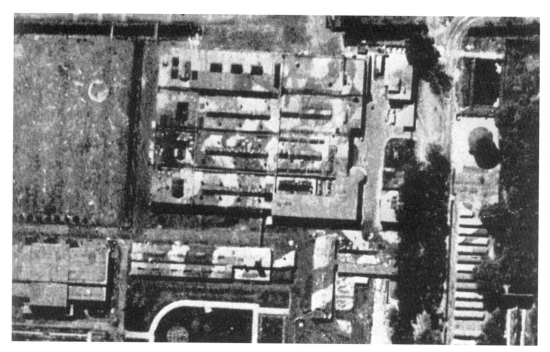

Before and after photographs showing the Focke-Wulf aircraft factory in Bremen, which produced the lethally effective Fw 190 fighter for the Luftwaffe; the factory was attacked by RAF bombers on the night of 25 June.

US Navy Douglas SBD Dauntless dive-bombers armed and ready on the deck of an aircraft carrier.

More Douglas Dauntless aircraft on the deck of a US Navy aircraft carrier, preparing to take off. During the Battle of Midway, four US Navy Dauntless squadrons attacked and sank or crippled all four of the fleet carriers in the Japanese force (*Akagi*, *Kaga*, *Soryu* and *Hiryu*).

A photograph showing the Battle of Midway at the end of June 1942. A US Navy aircraft carrier is seen surrounded by black puffs of smoke from anti-aircraft gunfire, with low-flying Japanese torpedo bombers to the left and right.

July

The first combat mission flown by the USAAF in Europe was a raid on German airfields in the Netherlands on 4 July, Independence Day. This photograph shows, from left to right: Sergeant Benny Cunningham; Sergeant Robert Golay; Lieutenant Randall Dorton; and Major Charles Kegelman. They were all decorated for their part in the raid, and are seen posing in front of the Boston bomber in which they flew.

A US-made Douglas Boston bomber in the Western Desert being prepared for a raid on an Axis position. The member of the ground crew in the foreground gives an idea of the size of the bomb waiting to be loaded into the Boston.

Opposite: An aerial photograph showing the strategically important city of Tobruk under attack; bombs can be seen exploding on two of the port's jetties to the top left of the photograph.

Soviet paratroopers on a mission to attack the supply routes behind the German lines. The upper image shows the paratroopers boarding their transport aircraft and the lower image shows one of the paratroopers landing. Interestingly, he is using a parachute with two canopies.

The Avro Lancaster, soon to become the backbone of RAF Bomber Command and one of the most famous British aircraft of the war, started to come into service in 1942. Powered by four Rolls-Royce Merlin engines, the Lancaster was reliable, safe and versatile.

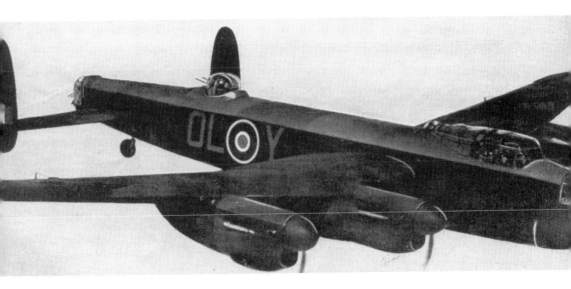

The exhibition halls on Berlin's Kaiserdamm are seen here covered in camouflage nets to prevent them from being spotted from the air and used as landmarks by bomber pilots.

Another photograph showing the use of camouflage in Berlin. This one shows one of the main east–west roads through Berlin, covered with camouflage netting and fake spruce trees in order to break up the lines of the road and prevent it being spotted from the air.

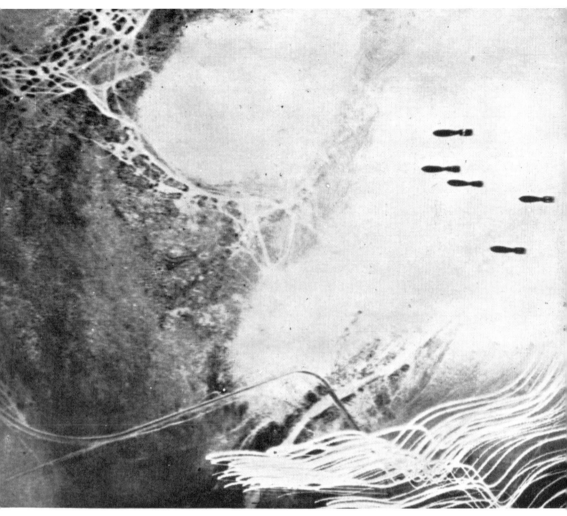

A bombing raid under way against an Axis airfield at Tmimi in Libya. The wavy lines in the bottom right of the photograph are caused by burning incendiary bombs on the ground.

Above: A flight of three Soviet air force bombers setting out to attack German forces in the valley of the River Don.

Left: An anti-aircraft gun crew on a battleship of the Soviet Black Sea Fleet escorting a convoy of ships carrying supplies. Fighting around the Black Sea was heavy during the summer of 1942 as the Germans pressed towards Stalingrad.

A convoy that had brought troops and supplies to the Australian forces fighting in New Guinea is seen coming under attack in the harbour from Japanese aircraft.

A house in Darwin, northern Australia, after having been hit by a Japanese bomb.

Trolleys loaded with incendiary bombs waiting to be delivered to aircraft taking part in the bombing of Hamburg on the night of 26/27 July.

A closer view of RAF ground crew handling a container in which rows of incendiary bombs can be seen. During the raid on 26/27 July, more than 400 aircraft dropped over 175,000 incendiaries, mostly damaging residential and semi-commercial areas of the city.

Smoke drifting across the Rhine from the customs house buildings at Düsseldorf. The city was subjected to area bombing by the RAF on the night of 31 July/1 August 1942, using a mixture of 4,000-lb high-explosive bombs, incendiaries and smaller explosive bombs to cause as much damage from fire as possible.

August

Anti-aircraft fire bursting in the air over Guadalcanal in the Solomon Islands as Japanese aircraft launched an attack on the force that landed on the island on 7 August.

Above: The island of Tulagi, also part of the Solomon Islands, following an attack by dive-bombers from a US Navy aircraft carrier.

Below: A map of the Solomon Islands, showing both Guadalcanal and Tulagi.

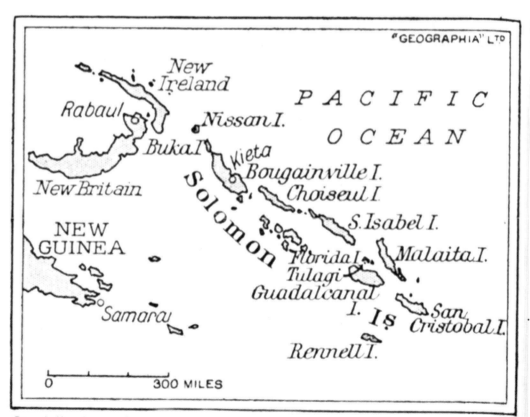

Specially drawn by "GEOGRAPHIA" LTD.

In early August, a convoy made its way through the Mediterranean to Malta and came under heavy attack from Axis aircraft as well as E-boats and submarines. This photograph shows a salvo of bombs falling near one of the merchant ships in the convoy.

Another view of the Malta convoy, showing bombs falling between two of the ships in the convoy. Known as Operation Pedestal, the convoy suffered considerable losses, with nine of fourteen merchant ships being sunk.

An artist's impression showing the most dangerous part of the journey to Malta, labelled here as 'Bomb Alley', between Sicily and the North African coast under German control.

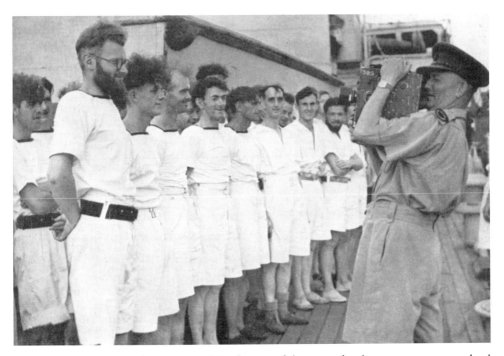

On 11 August, the aircraft carrier HMS *Eagle*, part of the escort for the convoy, was torpedoed by a U-boat. This photograph shows some of the survivors from the *Eagle* having their picture taken.

The Focke-Wulf Fw 190 was one of Germany's most effective aircraft designs. A captured Fw 190 can be seen in the upper photograph in RAF markings. In the photograph below, a group of engineers can be seen examining the cockpit, while the casing covering the engine has been removed, exposing the two 7.92 mm machine guns mounted on top of the engine.

Two photographs showing a tactic developed to counter German aerial attacks on convoys. The SS *Empire Tide* was a merchant ship fitted with a catapult and a Hurricane fighter, which could be launched to drive off or shoot down German bombers. After his flight, the pilot would abandon his aircraft and land in the sea, to be picked up by the convoy. Ships equipped with this system, first introduced in late 1941, were known as CAM (catapult aircraft merchantmen).

Left: Bomb damage to the Writing Room in the Cambridge University Union, caused during one of the final phases of Baedeker Raids carried out by the Luftwaffe.

Below: On 17 August, the first USAAF B-17 raid was carried out in Europe, an attack on the Sotteville railway yards at Rouen in Normandy. The raid was carried out by the 97th Bombardment Group, the first combat group of the Eighth Air Force to arrive in Britain.

Kanalhafen, an inland harbour to the north-west of the city of Osnabrück in the north-west of Germany, which was bombed on the night of 17 August. The target was a concentration of warehouses, dockside installations and a main railway goods station.

An Italian submarine surprised on the surface in the Mediterranean and attacked by a patrolling RAF Sunderland flying boat.

An unlucky sentry stands guard during a blizzard on an airfield in Alaska's Aleutian Islands, a base for patrols by US Navy aircraft, including the Catalina flying boat in the background, to watch against the Japanese. Two of the islands (Attu and Kiska) had been occupied by the Japanese in June.

September

The Battle of Stalingrad can be said to have begun on 3 September, as German troops entered the city's suburbs. The Germans had bombed the city heavily during the previous months, and this photograph, taken from a German aircraft, shows a bombing raid in progress against the shattered northern part of Stalingrad.

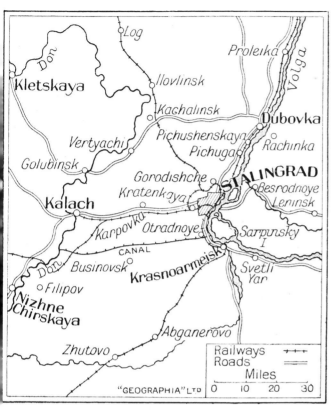

Two maps showing Stalingrad. The left map shows the city's position on the Volga, and the surrounding towns, while the right shows the city in more detail. Although the battle would be decided by the troops on the ground, German air power played a huge role in the assault on the city, providing close air support for the soldiers, bombing the city prior to the assault, attacking the flow of supplies from the eastern bank of the Volga and supplying the encircled German troops later in the battle.

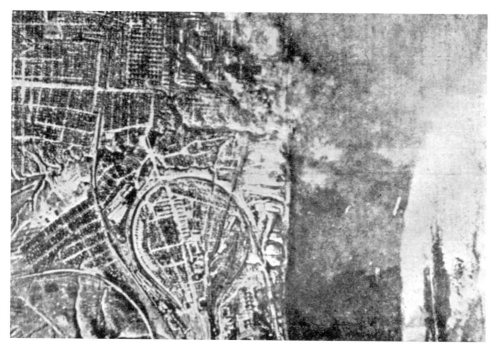

A German aerial photograph showing Stalingrad, with a large number of roofless houses visible as a result of the heavy bombardment of the city by aircraft and artillery.

A view of Stalingrad from the ground. The Germans began to advance on the city through July and August; there was a massive air raid on the city on 23 August and from then on, the city was under heavy air attack, which would intensify as air strikes were used to support the troops fighting in the city.

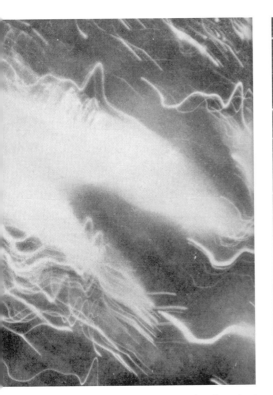 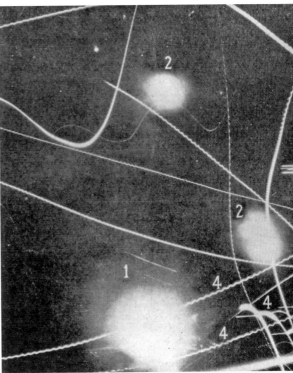

Above left: An eerie photograph taken during a night raid against the city of Karlsruhe, on the Rhine in the south-west of Germany, on 2 September.

Above right: Another photograph from the raid on Karlsruhe. 1: The flash of a 4,000-lb bomb exploding. 2: Anti-aircraft gunfire. 3: A fire burning on the ground. 4: Incendiary bombs.

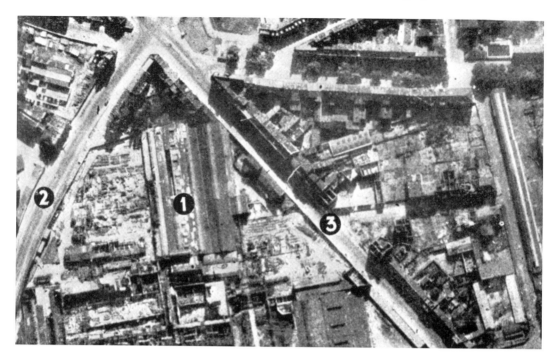

Two aerial reconnaissance photographs showing the city of Düsseldorf following an attack by the RAF on the night of 10/11 September. The photograph above shows the Thyssen Deutsche Roehren Werke steel plant, and the photograph below the area in and around the main railway station.

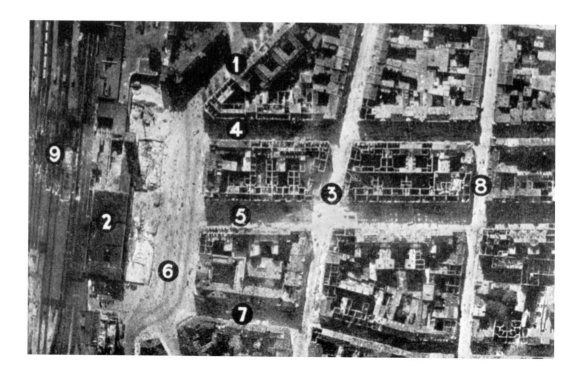

RAF air crew and ground crew pose in front of a Lancaster bomber following the raid on Düsseldorf on the night of 10/11 September.

The pilot, pipe firmly between his teeth, and two crew of a Coastal Command Lockheed Hudson pose in a hole in the wing made by a shell during an attack on a German convoy off the Dutch coast.

Before and after aerial reconnaissance photographs, showing the effect of a raid on the Focke-Wulf aircraft works at Neuenland, on the outskirts of Bremen in north-western Germany.

Above: The aircraft carrier USS
Wasp sinking after having been
hit by a Japanese torpedo off the
island of Guadalcanal, where she
had been providing air support for
the US troops fighting there.

Right: A delayed-action bomb
dropped in a Japanese air raid
explodes in New Guinea, where
Australian forces were fighting the
Japanese to retain control of Port
Moresby and prevent the Japanese
using it as a base for attacking
Australia.

Above: On 25 September, RAF Mosquito bombers attacked the Gestapo headquarters in occupied Oslo. A: A direct hit on the Gestapo building. B: Where the swastika flag had been flying. C: Oslo University.

Below: 'A' marks where the bombs were hitting the Gestapo building. Mosquitoes would become famous for highly accurate low-level bombing raids.

A spectacular photograph shows trucks highlighted against the skyline in the Western Desert by a storm of anti-aircraft fire as German aircraft attack an airfield. By the end of September 1942, Rommel's drive towards Alexandria and the Suez Canal had run out of steam in front of El Alamein, and Montgomery was preparing to drive Rommel back.

October

A Supermarine Seafire (short for 'Sea Spitfire') taking off from the deck of a Royal Navy aircraft carrier. A version of the Spitfire Mk VB adapted for naval service, the Seafire Mk Ib served with the Fleet Air Arm's 801 Squadron on HMS *Furious* from October 1942 to September 1944.

Soviet U2 aircraft flying over a pass in the northern Caucasus Mountains. The prototype of the U2 first flew in 1928; although outclassed by other aircraft of the time, the U2 was very effective in many roles, including as a night bomber, flying missions at very low altitude.

A Soviet anti-aircraft gun unit moving up to the front line in the northern Caucasus mountains. The area was strategically important because of the oilfields at the other end of the Caucasus, clustered around the city of Baku, now in Azerbaijan, on the Caspian.

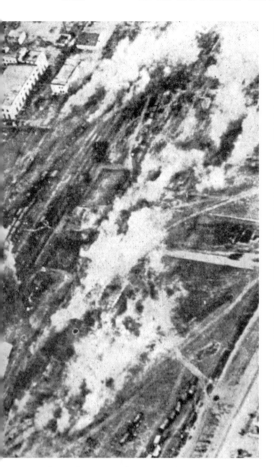 

Above left: Smoke rising from exploding bombs as Junkers Ju 87 Stuka dive-bombers attack Stalingrad's railway station.

Above right: The Soviet response to the constant Stuka attacks – a multi-barrelled anti-aircraft gun mounted on the back of a lorry.

US bomber pilots sit under the nose of one of their B-25 Mitchell bombers, planning the next mission against the Japanese forces around Port Moresby, New Guinea. In September, the Japanese were in sight of Port Moresby, but overextended their supply lines and had to go on the defensive.

Four pilots from the US Marine Corps who between them, according to the original caption of this photograph, accounted for forty Japanese aircraft in the skies over Guadalcanal and the Solomon Islands.

Left: On 21 October, B-17 Flying
Fortresses of the US Eighth Air Force
attacked the U-boat bases on the
French Atlantic coast at Lorient. In this
photograph, bombs can be seen just
leaving one of the aircraft. The massive
construction of the U-boat pens can be
seen on page 32.

Below: The king inspecting a B-17,
Holey Joe, the crew of which is lined up
beside their aircraft.

A map showing the Battle of El Alamein, in which the Eighth Army, under Bernard Montgomery, counter-attacked and drove back Rommel's Afrika Korps. Air power played a key role in the battle, attacking Axis communications, reserves and supplies.

Aircrew of the South African Air Force prepare to take off on a mission in support of the El Alamein offensive. Squadrons of the South African Air Force were a key part of the Desert Air Force that supported the Eighth Army.

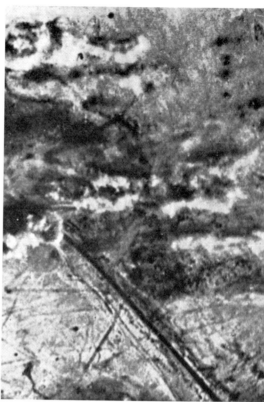

A raid by North American B-25 Mitchell bombers of the RAF as part of the El Alamein offensive. The left photograph shows the Mitchells dropping their bombs, while that on the right shows the bombs exploding on an airfield behind the German lines.

Opposite top: Part of a force of some ninety Lancaster bombers on their way to bomb the Schneider works in Le Creusot in Burgundy, eastern France. The Schneider works was a steel mill and major arms manufacturing centre, producing Schneider tanks, among other things.

Opposite middle: The Schneider works following the raid. This photograph shows damage to machine shops and sheds, as well as blast damage and derailed trucks.

Opposite bottom: On the night of 31 October, the Germans made a large-scale daylight attack against Canterbury, announcing that it was in retaliation for the RAF's raids against German cities. This photograph shows damage to houses in the city.

The wreckage of one of the nine aircraft that the defenders of Canterbury claim to have shot down during the raid.

The De Havilland Mosquito first began production in 1941, but only came into widespread service in 1942. One of the fastest operational aircraft in the world, it would start life as a high-altitude photograph reconnaissance aircraft, but in 1942 it would begin service as a high-speed bomber, and as a night fighter as well.

November

Tracer fire leaps up into the sky from anti-aircraft guns on British warships defending the Operation Torch landings in North Africa on 8 November. Much of the American force, some three divisions, was transported directly from the US by sea.

Another spectacular photograph of anti-aircraft guns firing at German aircraft, this time to defend Algiers, where a joint US-British force landed.

Another image of Algiers' defences against air attack. This photograph shows a smokescreen lying over the city to prevent the German bombers being able to spot their targets.

Grumman Martlet and Supermarine Seafire fighters on the deck of an aircraft carrier during the Operation Torch landings.

The aircraft carrier HMS *Argus* off the coast of North Africa. HMS *Argus* had started life as an Italian ocean liner, *Conte Rosso*, and had been purchased by the Admiralty and converted in 1916/17.

At the end of October, the aircraft carrier USS *Hornet*, from whose decks the Doolittle Raid had lifted off earlier in the year, was sunk in the Battle of the Santa Cruz Islands, during an attempt to stop a Japanese force reaching Guadalcanal.

US naval aircraft circle their aircraft carrier USS *Enterprise*, waiting to take their turn to land, following the Battle of the Santa Cruz Islands.

A convoy of US ships off Guadalcanal. The plume of smoke comes from a Japanese bomber attacking the convoy, which was shot down by the cruiser USS *San Francisco.*

A raid carried out by B-17 Flying Fortresses against Japanese shipping in the harbour at Rabaul in New Britain, off the west coast of the island of New Guinea.

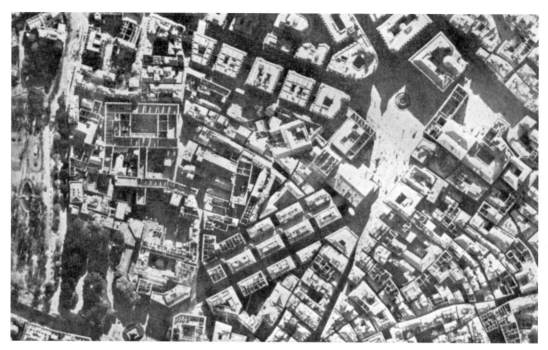

Photographs showing the effects of a bombing raid on the port of Genoa, in the north-west of Italy, on the night of 13/14 November.

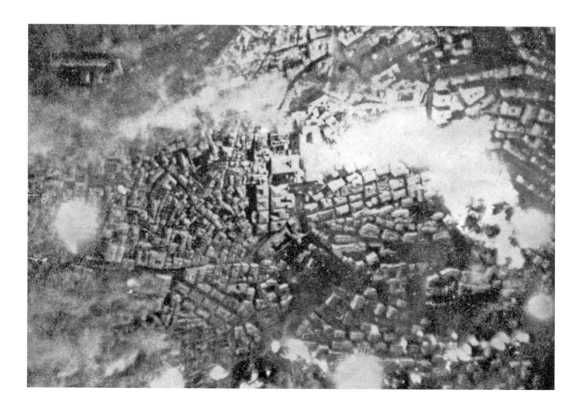

As the Afrika Korps retreated following the Battle of El Alamein, the RAF attacked the German forces. These attacks were made more effective by the limited choice of useable roads through the desert. This photograph shows an attack on the road between El Daba and Fuka.

A British transport column passes German vehicles wrecked in an air attack in the Halfaya Pass, strategically important as the only way through the steep escarpment south along the Libyan–Egyptian border from the coast.

When the weather was too bad to attack the usual targets in Germany, Bomber Command's crews would help out the Royal Navy by laying mines in the waters of occupied Europe. This photograph shows ground crew loading mines into the bomb bay of an Avro Lancaster named *Admiral Prune*.

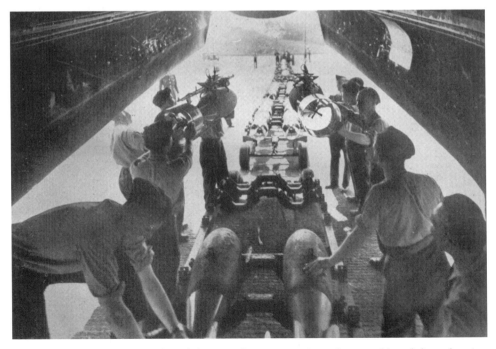

A photograph that gives an idea of the size of a Lancaster's unobstructed bomb bay, showing ground crew loading the aircraft with bombs.

A flight of Grumman TBF Avenger torpedo bombers. The Avenger, which started to come into service in summer 1942 and played a role in most of the major naval battles in the Pacific that year, had three crewmen, and could carry a 2,000-lb bomb or a torpedo in a bomb bay.

A boatload of survivors from a torpedoed merchant ship wave to a Coastal Command Sunderland flying boat. In autumn 1942, losses of shipping to U-boats had climbed again, after having dropped earlier in the war.

December

A Soviet bomber is prepared for a mission on a snow-covered airfield near Stalingrad. Soviet forces were able to help fighting during the bitter winter, while keeping the Germans besieged within the city.

WAAF barrage balloon operators undergoing training at the Balloon Training Unit, with an NCO instructor using a model balloon for demonstration purposes.

WAAF trainee barrage balloon operators watching as an RAF corporal demonstrates how to operate the winch used to raise and lower the balloons.

The view inside the cockpit of a Stirling. The first and second pilots are in their seats, looking back at the photographer, as the bomb aimer emerges from his compartment in the foreground.

A raid by Lockheed Ventura bombers, escorted by fighters, on the docks at Den Helder, north of Amsterdam, in the Netherlands on 23 December. The Ventura, a twin-engined bomber, was a development of the Hudson, and was purchased by Britain from the US as part of Lend-Lease.

A B-17 Flying Fortress of the Eighth Air Force taking off from an airbase somewhere in England. The squadrons of the 'Mighty Eighth' were based in the East Anglian counties of Suffolk, Norfolk and Cambridgeshire.

B-17s of the Eighth Air Force flying at high altitude, leaving vapour trails behind them. USAAF strategy was to bomb in daylight, from high altitude, with aircraft flying in tight formation so that they could protect each other from fighter attack.

Two photographs showing the aftermath of an air attack on a US Navy aircraft carrier in the Pacific. In the upper photograph, firefighting crews can be seen battling the flames caused by the explosion of a Japanese bomb. In the lower photograph, the crater in the carrier's wooden flight deck can be seen.

This photograph shows US warships under attack by Japanese aircraft off the coast of Guadalcanal, the sky speckled with black clouds of smoke from anti-aircraft fire.

The crew of this Short Stirling, N 3669, chalk up the sixty-second bombing on the aircraft's side. A tour lasted for thirty operations, and by 1943, only one in six were expected to survive their first tour.

A patrol of US Navy aircraft flying over the island of Midway. The Battle of Midway was one of the main events of the year, a key battle that tipped the balance of power in the Pacific away from the Japanese navy.

Scenes from the aircraft carrier HMS *Illustrious*. The image above shows the crew of one of *Illustrious*'s anti-aircraft guns, ready for action, while the image to the right shows an American-built Grumman Martlet fighter landing on the carrier. Martlet was the British name for the F4 Wildcat used by the US Navy on smaller escort carriers.

The bomber offensive continues. A flight of Handley Page Halifax bombers climbs through the clouds over Italy. As the Lancaster came into service in greater numbers, the Halifax and Short Stirling would see increasing use in Italy and the Mediterranean. Greater numbers of Lancasters would improve the ability of Bomber Command to launch devastating attacks, the scale and frequency of which would increase in 1943 as the bomber campaign grew, against German cities.